Pattern Sourcebook:
Chinese Style
250 Patterns for Projects and Designs

Shigeki Nakamura

BEVERLY MASSACHUSETTS

ROCKPORT PUBLISHERS

First published in the United States of America by
Rockport Publishers, a member of
Quayside Publishing Group
100 Cummings Center
Suite 406-L
Beverly, Massachusetts 01915-6101
Telephone: (978) 282-9590
Fax: (978) 283-2742
www.rockpub.com

ISBN-13: 978-1-59253-497-5
ISBN-10: 1-59253-497-X

10 9 8 7 6 5 4 3 2 1

Printed in Singapore

Preface

Chinese ornamental patterns are a developed form of art that has been influenced by the mixture of art that has traveled the Silk Road over the ages. The finest examples are wall paintings and statues in the Mogao Caves in Dunhuang, which are said to have been constructed in the days of Emperor Wu of Han more than 2,000 years ago. The caves were excavated over the course of more than a thousand years, starting in the mid-fourth century, by ten dynasties and sixteen countries.

The artwork of the Mogao Caves is in such an excellent condition that the caves have been called "a shrine of Buddhist art treasures."

Many artistic influences were transported along the Silk Road over the centuries, and they are found not only in Chinese arts, but also in Japanese art, craft, and architecture. The Chinese decorative art crafts achieved a flourishing zenith around the 1540s, during the Ming Dynasty. Assimilating unique carved lines with other elements of Buddhist art, the decorative art crafts created during this period—some featuring rich, bright colors—established the original Chinese style of patterns.

This book introduces Chinese ornamental patterns, specifically those created during the period mentioned above, when most traditional Chinese patterns originated. Many of the paintings of fortune and longevity—symbols such as the dragon, bird, phoenix, kirin (Chinese legendary creature in China), fish among seaweed, peach, pomegranate, grapes, loquat, shelf fungus, cherry, apple, peony, lotus flower, rose, floral scroll, and chrysanthemum—are rather mediocre in expression. Thus, we tend to fail to notice the real beauty of their decorative parts.

In this book, I excluded those paintings and selected only original Chinese-style patterns of all ages and organized them into eight chapters. I've also included a CD-ROM that features resources that you can apply to make your original patterns. I hope this book will be an important resource for your design work.

Shigeki Nakamura (Cobble collaboration)

Contents

How to use this book

[Explanatory notes]
● The dates of production of ornaments at "wooden architectural ornament" and some examples of architecture are unknown.
● The ornamental patterns at the Mogao Caves have been imitated by many painters in China. Some patterns clearly state the names of the caves they belong to (the 100th cave, for example), while others have no clues of their originals even if they are elaborately painted. Please understand that this book is focused on utility of patterns rather than historical background.
● Original Chinese names and pronunciations are translated into English. Words that have no English equivalents are listed in the term note below.
● The images in the attached CD-ROM are the same size, but some images in the book are trimmed to fit the layouts, and the colorings of some parts (i.e. background) has been changed.

Page Layout

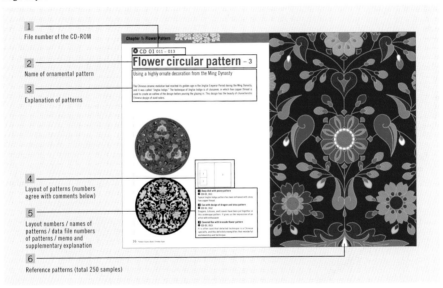

1
File number of the CD-ROM

2
Name of ornamental pattern

3
Explanation of patterns

4
Layout of patterns (numbers agree with comments below)

5
Layout numbers / names of patterns / data file numbers of patterns / memo and supplementary explanation

6
Reference patterns (total 250 samples)

Term note

Ban: Deep dish
Kan: Dish originally used to store pickles
Hei: Bottle used as a vase "瓶, hei/ping" has the same pronunciation with "平, peace" in Chinese and it is welcomed as a lucky item.
Gou: Vessel with lid, covered box
Ton: Chair of earthenware used outdoors
Kun: Incense burner
Kakoku: Vase that is narrow in the middle with decorated facet. "Koku" means a goblet.
Boutou: Hat box. Cylinder shaped earthenware to protect hats for rich people
Hakkko: Flower seal, a seal used for ornament of ancient earthenware
Seika: Porcelain painted with indigo-blue, Chinese cobalt

Chapter 1
Flower Pattern

● CD 01 001 – 003
Flower circular pattern – 1

Lotus, the flower of Buddhism, placed on the center of ceilings

This circular flower pattern is taken from mural and ceiling painting at the Mogao Caves in Dunhuang. Right in the center of Silk Road where Eastern and Western culture meet, different conceptions of beuty coexisted and combined. Let's imagine the artists who created the original designs of Chinese beauty from before the turn of the millenium.

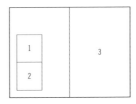

1 Ceiling painting, Center part ● CD 01_001
When we look at the whole painting, elements of Chinese design other than the simple peach-shaped lotus can be found in this pattern. They became established in later eras.

2 Ceiling painting, Center part ● CD 01_002
This bright pattern makes us wonder if there were kaleidoscopes in those days.

3 Ceiling painting, Center part ● CD 01_003
This may have been created a little later, as it seems to have been refined in form.

⦿ CD 01 004 – 006
Flower circular pattern – 2

Variation of same motif

The peach-shaped design in the Mogao Caves may be regarded more or less as the design that abstracted the lotus from the Buddhism flower. Various designs have been developed with detailed geometric composition, centering on this "Lotus flower circle." The pattern of the Center part of the ceiling painting has been taken from part of that flower and has been made to look simpler.

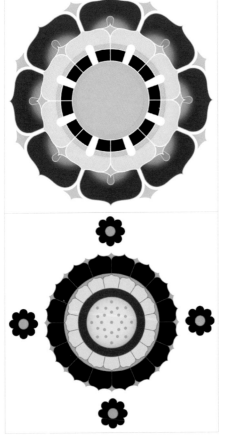

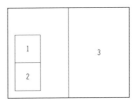

1 **Ceiling painting, center part** ⦿ CD 01_004
The artists must have been fascinated by the lines and patterns that appeared as a consequence of moving around the petals.

2 **Ceiling painting, center part** ⦿ CD 01_005
This design looks as if it has rings which were created by adding petals using a similar composition.

3 **Ceiling painting, center part** ⦿ CD 01_006
This composition has light, pleasant feeling and we are able to imagine the artists singing along while painting.

■ **Ceiling painting, center part** ● CD 01_007 The pattern of the outer circle has been excellently detailed. It would be a joy to design such a pattern.

■ **Ceiling painting, center part** ● **CD 01_008** This lotus flower has been designed using bold lines and color coded by geometrical pattern. It gives us a refreshing image of flowers.

■ **Border Ornament, Multiplied, Part** ◉ **CD 01_009** The hemicycle pattern has been laid alternately, and the lacing pattern has been overlapped in a circle. It shows us a form quite similar to the ceiling painting on the previous page.

■ **Border Ornament, Multiplied, Part** ● CD 01_010 This uses the same technique as the image on the previous page does. It is surprising that the artists had such flexibility and ability to design using a given motif depending on the purpose and space for different images.

● CD 01 011 – 013

Flower circular pattern – 3

Using a highly ornate decoration from the Ming Dynasty

The Chinese ceramic evolution had reached its golden age in the Jingtai Emperor Period during the Ming Dynasty, and it was called "Jingtai Indigo." The technique of Jingtai Indigo is of cloisonné, in which fine copper thread is used to create an outline of the design before pouring the glazing in. This design has the beauty of characteristic Chinese design of vivid colors.

1	3
2	

1 Deep dish with peony pattern
● CD 01_011
Typical Jingtai Indigo pattern has been enframed with shiny fine copper thread.

2 Can with design of dragon and lotus pattern
● CD 01_012
Dragons, Lotuses, and Leaves have been put together in this arabesque pattern. It gives us the impression of an artist with enthusiasm.

3 Covered Box with brocade flower pattern
● CD 01_013
It is often said that detailed technique is a Chinese specialty, and this definitely exemplifies their wonderful workmanship and technique.

■ **Floral Scroll, Tang Dynasty** ● CD 01_014 In Tang Dynasty patterns, flowers are usually linked together symmetrically. This dimensional floral scroll pattern has charm in its form.

■ **Buddha's Image, Nimbus Part** ● CD 01_015 This is a part of a Nimbus drawn on the wall as the background of a Buddha's image in Mogao Cave. A concentric circle is drawn with the string of the wave pattern for this elegant and rhythmical image of a spreading aureole.

⊙ CD 01 016 – 020
Ornament – 1

Similarity in flower patterns - ornaments for old wooden architecture in China and Japan

When a new lifestyle is introduced, it brings with it a different sense of beauty that adjusts to the climate and people. It also brings new culture and technology due to the exchange of people. Buddhism was introduced to Japan from China in 6th century and the world's oldest existing example of wooden architecture, Horyu Temple, was built then. We are able to find similar qualities in the architectural ornaments of China and Japan as a consequence of this cultural contact.

1		
2		5
3		
4		

1 **Peony pattern in wood carving** ⊙ CD 01_016
It would be difficult to differentiate this from Japanese wood-carved craftwork if Japanese-style coloring were put to this design.

2 **Peony pattern in wood carving** ⊙ CD 01_017
When we look at these two designs, we are able to understand the sense of beauty of the Japanese artists.

3 **Peony pattern in wood carving** ⊙ CD 01_018
The style of this peony gives us the impression that it is actually a Japanese peony pattern.

4 **Peony pattern in wood carving** ⊙ CD 01_019
This part of a peony painting is used for Chinese fabric in Japan.

5 **Wall painting of wooden pagoda** ⊙ CD 01_020
It is not very clear due to the old document, but this pattern seems to be an iron painting three dimensionally drawn on a solid plaster wall (colored).

● CD 01 021 – 024
Ornament – 2

Flower pattern for architecture ornament with a slightly different sense of beauty from the Japanese

It is said that the oldest wooden Temple of Confucius (pinyin: Kǒng miào), a temple devoted to the memory of Confucius, was built in 450 BC. The oldest surviving wooden architecture of China is Nanchan Monastery on Mount Wutai, which was built in 782 CE. We are able to find design elements in the decoration of those buildings that were inherited from ancient times.

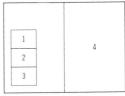

1 Ornament of wooden architecture (Chinese flower)
● CD 01_021
We find slightly incongruity in the form of flower and the way the leaves are laid out.

2 Ornament of wooden architecture (Chinese flower)
● CD 01_022
This is the composition of the flowers that could be found on the sides of the pedestal of the Buddhist image.

3 Ornament of wooden architecture (Chinese flower)
● CD 01_023
This is the same composition as above. It gives us an impression of Buddhist painting, although the design of the flower has a sense of incongruity.

4 Wall painting of wooden architecture (Floral Scroll, Tang Dynasty)
● CD 01_024
The design of the former era, Sui Dynasty, is abstract, and some of it does not look like the floral scroll pattern. The design of the Tang Dynasty is more familiar to us.

● CD 01 025 – 027
Ornament – 3-1

The typical Chinese decoration pattern in Chinese ceramic

"Jingdezhen" and "Jingtai Indigo" ceramics reached their golden age during the Ming Dynasty in China. They have a diverse range of patterns. In particular, flower patterns are often seen in the decoration of "Jingtai Indigo." What is special about it is the abstraction of the design and the imagination of the artists. Because they are not ordinary dishes, the unmistakable influence of distinctive Chinese style can be found in these.

1	3
2	

1 Covered jar, part ● CD 01_025
There is a unique affected atmosphere in this. The repeated pattern increases this atmosphere.

2 Triangle vase, part ● CD 01_026
Taking a look at just this pattern reminds us of nobility. It makes us think that this bottle would have been used in the Imperial Court.

3 Bottle with painted design of phoenix, part
● CD 01_027
This flower pattern is designed from an image of the wings of a Phoenix after extracting a part of a complicated Phoenix design.

■ Cup with painted design of peony, part ● CD 01_028

◎ CD 01 029 – 032

Ornament – 3-2

National character in Chinese ceramic art and architecture ornament

The techniques of gilding and silver plating were already developed in 450-220 B.C. for design in bronze ware and the stone cavern fresco group, and it has been succeeded in the various Chinese civilizations in years later. Craftsmen from western regions imitated and gave influence to them, and together they developed the original beauty of Chinese "national character."

1	4
2	
3	

1 Square vase, part
◎ CD 01_029
This is more like a Chinese paper-cutting design which has the common touch and yet it is a distint design.

2 Cup with painted design of lotus, part
◎ CD 01_030
The Chinese lotus design is often symmetric, as in this pattern.

3 Cup with painted design of lotus and bird, part
◎ CD 01_031
The set of exuberant lines are lively, and unlike those common lotus designs, this is bold yet elegant.

4 Bottle with painted design of red star lily, part
◎ CD 01_032
It shows the unity of Chineseness. The lilies are not exactly splendid but almost sensual, and both the buds and leaves are drawn mysteriously here.

■ **Ornament of wooden pagoda** ◉ **CD 01_033**   This design has taken in joyful flowers and birds that seek for happiness. There is not an inconsistency in the form of outer frame.

■ **"Ton" chair painted with design of lotus flower, part** ◉ **CD 01_034** As a Chinese traditional lotus design, this is the most commonly used pattern. But it also means that this can be used as a basic pattern to many other designs.

■ **Ornament of wooden pagoda, part** ◉ **CD 01_035** This is a comparatively simple design and slightly bland. However it shows the artist's willingness to make this pattern more unique.

Chapter 2
Animal Pattern

● CD 02 036 – 039
Dragon pattern – 1

The pattern of dragon that has the most significance in China

Many legends of dragons are still told and alive after 4000 years of Chinese history. The dragon is regarded as a holy, lucky sign and a symbol of happiness who shares respect and affection with people in China. It has also been used as symbol for marine transportation and at annual festivals to keep evil spirits away.

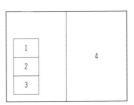

1 **Facet of vase with painted design of dragon**
● CD 02_036
Simple expression using similar techniques of single brush strokes gives softer impression to the imposing dragon. This is very much a familiar design.

2 **Bottle in the shape of a gourd with painted design of zodiac and flower, neck part**
● CD 02_037
A precise design of two dragons facing each other is creating an interesting continuous pattern in this.

3 **Dish with painted design of dragon, frame part**
● CD 02_038
This is excellently balanced with the simplified pattern of two dragons facing each other using color red and the flaming red of the treasure ball effectively.

4 **Vase with pattern of dragon, center part**
● CD 02_039
The dragon patterns of the Jingtai Indigo Era are often designed with their wings and legs emerging as clouds of heavens.

■ **Covered box with painted design of dragon and scroll, center part** ◉ CD 02_040 It is written in the literature that the wings of the dragon eventually changed into flame as time went on. This pattern represents the sacredness of the flame using the figure of the dragon.

■ **Can with painted design of dragon and lotus, center part** ◉ CD 02_041 The charm of this design is that it managed to put the dragon and lotus together with arabesque.

■ **Can with painted design of dragon and grass scroll, center part** ◉ **CD 02_042** This grass and dragon design uses treasure gem to resemble a lotus and makes it look like flame. This is a good example of the background of these legendary materials becoming a design consideration.

● CD 02 043 – 045
Dragon pattern – 2

As a symbol of the Emperor, the dragon rises above every animal

In China, they call the first Emperor of Tai a "dragon's ancestor", the features of the forefather of Han a "dragon's face", and the body of the Emperor the "body of dragon". The dragon was considered as the symbol of noble families, so common people were not allowed to use the pattern of dragon. The designs of dragons for Emperors were drawn as five-fingered dragons and the common people were allowed the dragon design only when it was four or three-fingered. As a result of this, the designs of dragons started to develop.

| 1 | 3 |
| 2 | |

1 Hat box with a painted design of a dragon in a circular pattern, center part
● CD 02_043
"The corps of dragon" is a pattern, designed to be round in shape. The reason for this design being subtle is that all the little parts have been carefully detailed.

2 Facet of a vase with a painted design of a dragon, part
● CD 02_044
A dragon with scales is called a "biting dragon". It looks frightening, but at the same time it is humorously drawn.

3 Round dish with a painted design of dragons and grass scrolls, center part
● CD 02_045
This design has the sophistication of the rising dragon, des-

■ "Ton" chair with the painted designs of Four Symbols, Blue Dragon part ● CD 02_046

This is the dragon from the design of Four Symbols. Four Symbols are Blue Dragon (east/blue), White Tiger (west/white), Phoenix (south/red) and the Turtle Snake (north/black).

● CD 02 047 – 049
Phoenix pattern

The imaginary sacred bird the phoenix, subsistent in design

Phoenix patterns have also been used in Japan, where they are called "Paulownia, Bamboo, and Phoenix patterns". This is based on the legend that the Chinese Phoenix does not live anywhere but in paulownia tree, does not eat anything else but bamboo, and only drinks spiritual spring water. It is also said it lives by itself, when it flies others follow, and brings a peaceful world. Perhaps because this legendary spiritual creature possesses all the desire of people, the phoenix has been portrayed as realistic bird in design.

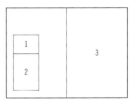

1 Round incense burner with a painted design of a phoenix, part
● CD 02_047
This exotic design is no doubt a Chinese pattern inherited from the Silk Road.

2 "Ton" chair with a painted design of Four Symbols, Blue Dragon part
● CD 02_048
This Tang-era phoenix is not just colored with three colors (green, brown, navy), as it often is. This richly colored Phoenix comes from the story that the bird sings in five different voices.

3 Vase with a painted design of a phoenix
● CD 02_049
With its refined expression using different shades of Indigo, this phoenix may be singing of the purity of life.

■ **"Ton" chair with the painted designs of Four Symbols, Phoenix part** ⊙ CD 02_050 When the dragon is a symbol of an Emperor, the phoenix becomes a symbol of an Empress. This design has true elegance.

⊙ CD 02 051 – 054

Peacock Pattern

The bird of fortune competes for its beauty and legend with the phoenix

It is regarded as an auspicious bird that teaches us "Nine Virtues" (to be generous and strict, to be obedient but firm, etc.), and also as a symbol of wealth and honor. Since it is such a beautiful bird, it has been thought of as the bird of paradise. The peacock in his pride has the true beauty to contribute to design based on the legend.

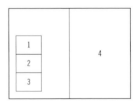

1 Jar with a painted design of a peacock, part
⊙ CD 02_051
This peacock design is a rather simple one. It has been designed to fill up a gap in the main structure of the design.

2 Jar with a painted design of a peacock, part
⊙ CD 02_052
This extensively detailed design represents the beauty of the peacock.

3 Jar with a painted design of a peacock, part
⊙ CD 02_053
We can learn from the picture above that this is the part of the peacock's rectrix. The arabesque pattern has been used here to give it Chinese style.

4 Jar with a painted design of a peacock, part
⊙ CD 02_054
The peacock is regarded as the bird of paradise in legends, so this has been designed as if it were the crest to be put up on the paradise gate.

⊙ CD 02 055 – 057
Butterfly Pattern

Chinese "curved" design is the world's common theme for designs.

The word "Butterfly" in both China and Japan has the same pronunciation as the word "length", and it has been applied to various designs to wish for longevity. The beauty and charm of butterflies as they fly and flutter is an important motif all around the world. The original Chinese design would be in curved lines of scrolls in the butterfly patterns.

1	3
2	

1 Ornament of a wooden pagoda, part
⊙ CD 02_055
An elegant composition of the butterfly on the corner looking at the flowers on both sides creates a sophisticated image.

2 Bottle with a painted design of a butterfly and a flower
⊙ CD 02_056
This is a peculiar design of a flame-like butterfly put in the frame of a referee's fan.

3 Bottle with a painted design of a butterfly and a flower
⊙ CD 02_057
In Chinese designs like this one, the butterfly has many linear patterns of trailing plants.

■ **Bottle with a painted design of a butterfly and a flower** ● CD 02_058 The arabesque design drawn on the right and left of the butterfly is probably replicate of the wings. However, the design could be completed without them.

■ **Bottle with a painted design of a butterfly and a flower** ● CD 02_059 This design has a mysterious atmosphere with the elegant composition of the fluttering butterfly against the rich indigo background color.

Chapter 3
Linear Pattern

● CD 03 060 – 062
Linear flower pattern – 1

The representative example of Chinese pattern that changes with time

Designs change with time anywhere. There are very many border decoration patterns in China and, as they represent different eras, they are very diverse. On the whole, tendencies in Chinese design have moved from geometrical patterns with subtle colors to various arabesque patterns, and the color scheme gradually became vivid and bold.

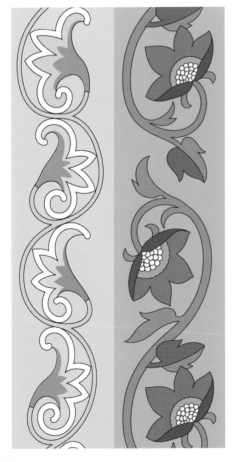

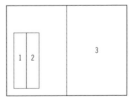

1 2 3 Ornament of wooden pagoda, part
● CD 03_060, 061, 062
These linear flower patterns join together like arabesque pattern. This is a design with flexible form that could be used with any different Buddhism flowers.

■ **Border ornament** ● CD 03_063

■ **Border ornament** ● CD 03_064

The Sixteen Kingdom existed during the Jin Dynasty, which was 300 years before Sui Dynasty. The Tang Dynasty came 100 years after the Sui Dynasty.

■ **Border ornament** ◉ CD 03_065   ■ **Border ornament** ◉ CD 03_066

It's hard to distinguish the different styles used in these 300 years. Some of them are not all that different.

● CD 03 067 – 070
Linear flower pattern – 2

The unexpected beauty of single flower design made into a continuous pattern

Linear pattern means a line drawn at a fixed interval. In design, linear pattern means the decoration created along the line. We are able to find the Chinese style curved lines in a flower pattern when we look at the running pattern on ancient architecture and the rim of craft potteries.

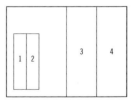

1 2 Ornament of wooden pagoda, part
● CD 03_067, 068
These patterns can be found on beams and the horizontal pieces of timber on walls. They were drawn or carved and then colored.

3 4 Covered box with painted design of brocade flower pattern
● CD 03_069, 070
This delicate pattern is not at all a strange design to us. It is a relatively universal design.

■ Ornament of wooden pagoda, part ● CD 03_071

■ Covered box with a painted design of three sheep, Part ● CD 03_073

■ Square vase, part ● CD 03_074

■ **Square vase, part** ● **CD 03_075** Compared with the previous design, this one has more of a Chinese flavor.

■ **Vase in square pyramid shape, part** ● **CD 03_076** This is a composition of a flower, leaf and stalk. The Chinese element is standing out more than the design of the flower.

● CD 03 077 – 080
Linear flower pattern – 3

Effective use of gold outline harmonizing the colors

The patterns of Jingtai Indigo design are outlined. Those vases are put in fire, and the outlines come out glowing in gold. The color gold not only attracts attention, but it brings out all other colors harmoniously and even luxuriously. The expression of a design changes depending on how effectively this gold lining is used. It would be interesting to focus on this characteristic Chinese gold lining without the effect of peculiar Chinese colors on designs.

1	
2	4
3	

1 Bottle with a painted design of peony pattern, part
● CD 03_077
This design is slightly abstract but has interesting use of linear that matches the shape of a peony.

2 Bottle with a painted design of a lotus, part
● CD 03_078
This is the method that by placing different colors on each lotus pattern avoids dull impressions.

3 Bottle with painted design of a peony pattern, part
● CD 03_079
This design has unusual design and color.

4 Vase in a square pyramid shape, part
● CD 03_080
This is very much an authentic Chinese design.

■ **Bottle with a painted design of two phoenixes** ● CD 03_081 This probably represents gingko leaves. The color and the shape are very beautiful.

■ **Stem cup, dish part** ● CD 03_082 This design is elegant and has a female touch.

■ **Square vase, part** ● **CD 03_083** Flower design.

■ **Triangle vase, bottle part** ● **CD 03_084** It gives us the impression that it has been improvised and came out as a flower pattern.

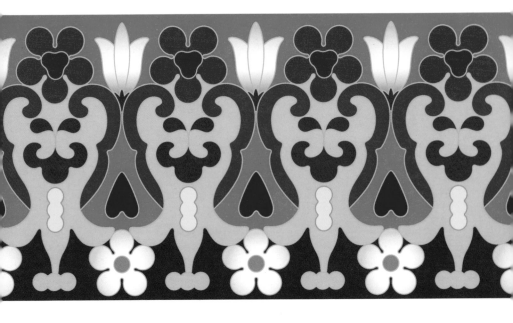

■ **Bottle with a painted design of "Hakko" flower seal, part** ● CD 03_085 It would be interesting to take out a small part of this design.

■ **Vase with a painted design of golden-rayed lily, part** ● CD 03_086 It doesn't necessarily mean that you need a rambunctious design to make it Chinese.

■ **Vase with a painted design of golden-rayed lily, part** ● CD 03_087   Is it intentional that the pattern appears to look like a face?

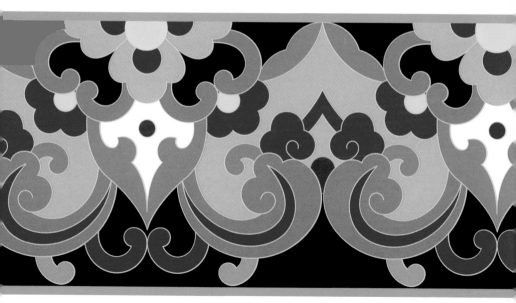

■ **Bottle with a painted design of phoenix, part** ● CD 03_088   Well-made composition shows this is the country where arabesque pattern was invented and developed.

● CD 03 089 – 092

Linear patterns of floral arabesque* and graphic pattern – 1

The charm of architectural ornaments without colors

Originally, the paints on royal palace architecture and ornamental linear patterns on pagodas were designed to make them look gorgeous and beautiful. However, when we look at the graceful curvilinear patterns it brings out the uniqueness of Chinese decoration that could be enjoyed in monochrome color.

*floral arabesque: Chinese grass and flower motif, or foliage-scroll patterns of flowers and leaves.

1	
2	4
3	

1 2 3 Ornament of wooden pagoda, Part
● CD 03_089, 090, 091
There are several varieties of ornamental style for wooden architectures: openwork carving, wood carving, colors on woodcarving, plaster relief, etc. And they can be seen on many places, such as transoms, walls, stair handrails, railings, and beams.

4 Ornament of wooden pagoda, Part
● CD 03_092
This design is simple yet bold, with very detailed geometric patterns.

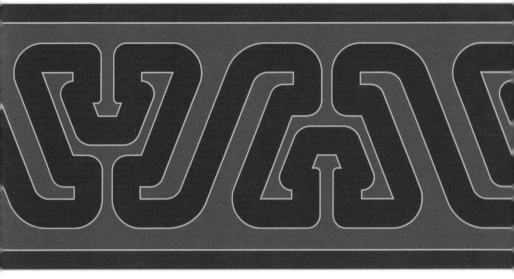

■ **Ornament of wooden pagoda, part** ● **CD 03_093** This is a simple pattern which is a very suitable decoration for architecture.

■ **Ornament of wooden pagoda, part** ● **CD 03_094** This is a detailed and refined design that symbolizes nobleness and wealth.

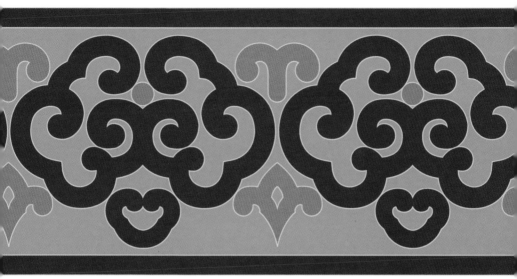

■ Ornament of wooden pagoda, part ● CD 03_095

◉ CD 03 096 – 098

Linear patterns of floral arabesque and graphic pattern – 2

Flexible thinking on the design for borders and the technique to develop them

There is a variety of border patterns in China, from geometric to representational arabesque designs. It teaches us to develop and design with a flexible mind unconstrained by the traditional Chinese composition techniques. These patterns were developed and woven with that technique, and they give us a lot of ideas for designs.

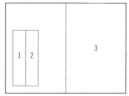

1 2 Ornament of wooden architecture
◉ CD 03_096, 097
It is not known when these works were created. However, we can easily find the excellent craftsmanship in them.

3 Ceiling paintings at the Mogao Caves, Part
◉ CD 03_098
This is a beautiful linear pattern which has been extracted from ceiling paintings at the Mogao Caves.

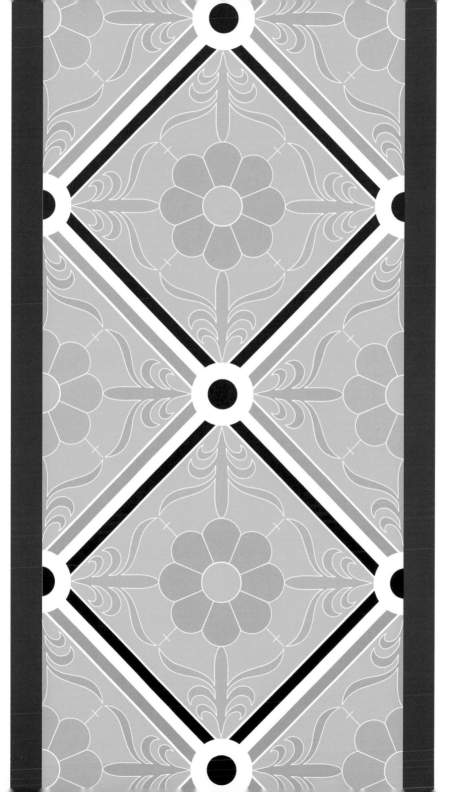

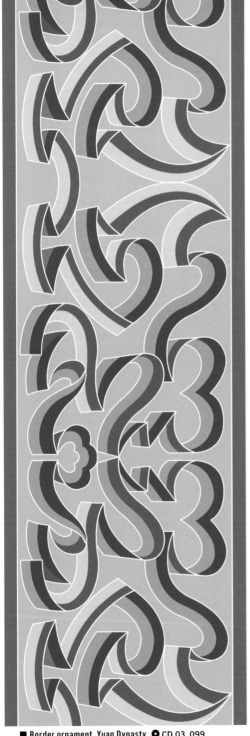

■ Border ornament, Yuan Dynasty ● CD 03_099

■ Border ornament, Northern Zhou Dynasty ● CD 03_100

■ Border ornament ● CD 03_101

● CD 03 102 – 105
Linear patterns of floral arabesque and graphic pattern – 3

The linear pattern that supports the background and does not join in the center part of the design

This is a decoration pattern of "Jingtai Indigo," explained in Linear Flower Pattern-3, and the name of the design derives from the central pattern of the design. This is one example of many designs in which the central pattern is divided into two totally different linear designs.

1 2 3 4 Bottle with painted design of peony
● CD 03_102, 103, 104, 105
It is just like listening to music and hearing the unique harmony of individual voices.

■ Old seismometer, part ● CD 03_106

■ Bottle, Chengde Mountain Resort, part ● CD 03_107

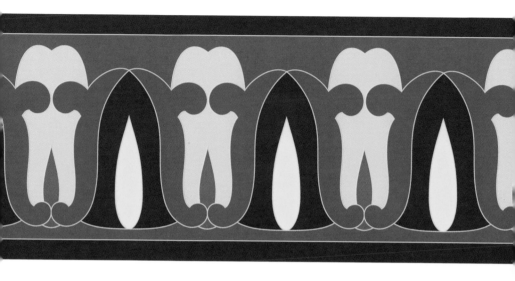

■ Can with painted design of lotus scroll ● CD 03_108

■ Hat box with painted design of lotus, part ● CD 03_109

● CD 03 110 – 113
Linear patterns of floral arabesque and graphic pattern – 4

Linear patterns to divide central pattern has a secret of Chinese "forms"

Ancient Chinese vessels were created in a variety of forms; some are in gourd shapes, some are narrow in the middle, neck, or leg part, and others have handles. As I mentioned in the preceding section "Linear patterns of floral arabesque and graphic pattern – 3", some linear patterns are very different from the center part ones. Still, those linear patterns have certain similarity in their forms, and that will be a key to understanding the Chinese style of forms.

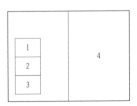

1 2 3 4 Three layers, covered box, part
● CD 03_110, 111, 112, 113
When creating linear patterns, there should always be a sensibility cultivated by history and tradition.

■ Four Symbols*, "Ton" chair, part ● CD 03_114

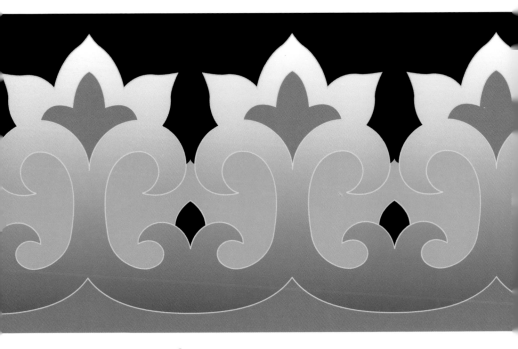

■ Four Symbols*," Ton" chair, part ● CD 03_115

*Four Symbols : shishin(Ch: sishen). Ancient Chinese mythical creatures associated with the four cardinal directions.

■ Bottle with a painted design of a lotus, part, Ming Dynasty   ● CD 03_116

■ Bottle with a painted design of a chrysanthemum, part   ● CD 03_117

⦿ **CD 03** 118 – 121

Linear patterns of floral arabesque and graphic pattern – 5

Various curved lines to decorate Chinese ornaments

Each Linear pattern in this section is a simple unit. When repeating a unit motif in a circular or a lined form to make a linear pattern, curved lines and the whole composition are important. The Chinese linear patterns are composed of various shapes of curves, and still they are successful as a whole design. We have much to learn from this technique.

1	4
2	
3	

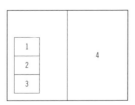

■1 ■2 ■3 ■4 **Bottle with painted design of phoenix, Part**
⦿ CD 03_118 119 120 121
Although the patterns appear unexplained, there is indescribable harmony in them.

■ Bottle with a painted design of a phoenix, part ● CD 03_122

■ Hat box with a painted design of a lotus, part ● CD 03_123

Chapter 4
Frame Pattern

● CD 04 124 – 127
Floral arabesque

The idea of "团*(dan, tuan)" (circle, sphere) created the Chinese form of frame patterns

In China, circular ornamental pattern is called "团(dan, tuan)" (circle, sphere). A continuous repetition of pattern represents eternity, family heredity, and posterity. After all, the unique Chinese frame patterns, which produce continuous circular designs, are symbols of everlasting fortune to the Chinese people.

* The pronunciation of "团" is "tuan" in Chinese. It means a circle or sphere.

1	
2	4
3	

1 Wall ornament of a wooden pagoda
● CD 04_124
This design has similarity to the patterns of ancient Europe.

2 Three Layers, covered box, part
● CD 04_125
Chinese grass (floral arabesque) is also called Ting grass.

3 "Ton" chair painted in the Ting style with a painted design of a phoenix, part
● CD 04_126
This adopts a refined and elegant floral arabesque pattern.

4 Bottle with a painted design of a zodiac pattern, part
● CD 04_127
Combinations of motifs divide into many frame patterns.

■ **Deep dish with five fortune pattern, part** ● CD 04_128 This is a superb example of intricate frame ornament.

■ **Covered box with a painted design of three sheep, part** ● CD 04_129 Though difficult to understand, the design has exquisite elegance.

■ **Deep dish with five fortune pattern, part** ● CD 04_130 This motif seems to have a hidden meaning beyond our imagination.

■ **Bottle with a painted design of a pine tree and a crane, part** ● CD 04_131 This is a well-designed pattern. It is regrettable that a poor painting is inside the frame.

■ **Incense burner with a painted design of a floral scroll, part** ● **CD 04_132** The small design in the frame is incomprehensi-

■ **Facet of a vase with a painted design of the zodiac, part** ● CD 04_133 The clear outline stands out sharply.

● CD 04 134 – 137
Graphic pattern

While expressing fortune, the designs show harmonized "complexity"

It is simple to put a single unit repeatedly in a circle form and use it as frame pattern. On the other hand, to put complicated elements in harmony with each other is a rather difficult task. Furthermore, to make it function as a lucky symbol, which means it is acceptable to anyone, is far more difficult.

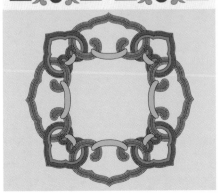

1	4
2	
3	

1 Ornament of a wooden pagoda, part
● CD 03_134
This is a simple but tricky composition.

2 Cigarette tool, part
● CD 03_135
Without the flowers in the center, this pattern looks very contemporary.

3 Ceiling painting, part
● CD 03_136
Combined small and large shapes in a chain give the motif an additional meaning.

4 Covered box in five-petals-shape, part
● CD 03_137
This has unique design even in the details.

■ **Screen, part** ● CD 04_138   This is only a part of the screen, but we can imagine the magnificent whole.

● CD 04 139 – 142
Creature

Techniques of frame patterns composed of typical lucky symbols.

There are a great number of lucky patterns in China. We have no idea why bats and butterflies are lucky symbols. One reason could be pronunciation; for example, the Chinese pronunciation of butterfly "蝶di-e" sounds the same as "耋 di-e," which means 80 years old.

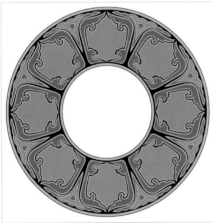

	3
1	
2	4

1 Bottle with a painted design of bats, part
● CD 04_139
The bats and painting inside show a mysterious world.

2 Round dish with a painted design of dragons and grass scrolls, part
● CD 04_140
This peacock motif itself makes a poor impression. It is one of the elements used to fill space.

3 Vase with a painted design of a "Hakko" flower seal, part
● CD 04_141
The bats are arranged in an interesting shape.

4 Facet of a vase with a painted design of a zodiac pattern
● CD 04_142
This is a beautiful Chinese original pattern with hidden phoenixes.

⊙ CD 04 143 – 145
Flower

Interesting frame patterns of flowers with meanings

The traditional flower patterns in China are the lotus and the peony. These flowers, including their leaves, are painted in various excellent patterns.

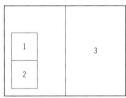

1	3
2	

1 Ceiling painting, center part ⊙ CD 04_143
This is a variation on the lotus motif. It is well composed of the same kind of motifs.

2 Hat box, lid part ⊙ CD04_144
Strange motifs of large and small peonies arranged in a circle give a tight impression.

3 "Ton" chair with a painted design of a phoenix painted in the Ting style, part ⊙ CD 04_145
This has an elegant and noble composition, which suits the image of peony.

■ **Wall ornament of wooden pagoda** ● CD 04_146
The same pattern can be seen in Japanese Buddhist temples and
Shinto shrines.

■ **Wall ornament of wooden pagoda** ● CD 04_147
The main motif of the lotus means narrowness, while the sub-
jective frame means width.

■ **Bottle with a painted design of a peony pattern, part** ● CD 04_148 Intricate motifs are arranged in a simple but elegant
design.

Chapter 5
Cloud Pattern

⊙ CD 05 149 – 152
Cloud

Fortune telling cloud takes a supporting part in ornament.

It seems that the cloud pattern in China is a secondary theme, seldom painted as a main pattern. Almost all the cloud patterns appear as combinations with dragons. It is probably because both dragon and cloud are regarded as lucky motifs.

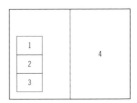

1 Carved wooden ornament of a pagoda, part
⊙ CD 05_149
This is to decorate the overhead beams.

2 Bottle with a painted design of a dragon pattern, part
⊙ CD 05_150
Consecutive motifs are efficiently lined.

3 Facet vase with painted design of dragon pattern, Part
⊙ CD 05_151
Tiling clouds around a dragon have humorous shapes.

4 Buddha's Image, Nimbus, center part
⊙ CD 05_152
This solid composition has space effect for halos.

■ **Vase with a painted design of an auspicious dragon and clouds in water, part** ● CD 05_153 The pattern does not seem to be in order, but with a dragon appearing on the top, it will be well-balanced.

■ **Pot with a painted design of an auspicious cloud pattern, part** ● CD 05_154 The design and coloring express auspicious clouds well.

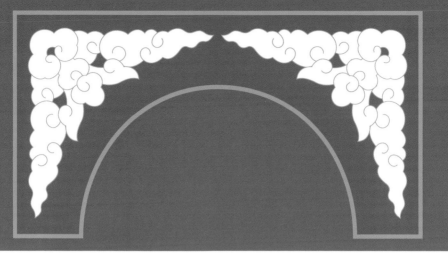

■ **Carved wooden gate of a pagoda, part** ● CD 05_155 Clouds were often used as ornaments on corners.

■ **Carved wooden ornament of pagodas** ● CD 05_156 This seems to be a wooden carving. The tiling of auspicious clouds conveys an atmosphere of fortune.

■ **Ceiling painting, center part** ● **CD 05_157** Geometric patterns of clouds spread in every direction around this.

■ **Ceiling painting, center part** ● **CD 05_158**

Chapter 6
Character Pattern

● **CD 06** 159 – 162

Longevity (Kotobuki, Shou)

Lucky symbol characters from ancient times to wish happiness

The Chinese people have a philosophical concept of happiness as "five fortune". 寿 comes first among the five lucky symbols. 寿, which means "longevity," is a typical example of Chinese lucky symbol characters. Next follows "Wealth", and "Health" comes in the third. This concept and tradition of "five fortune" is believed to have started in ancient times. Presumably, the regular use of lucky sign characters started in the Tang Dynasty (around 600 A.D.).

1	4
2	
3	

1 Large dish with "Shou" character in dragon and lotus scroll pattern ● CD 06_159

2 Pot with "Shou" character in auspicious cloud pattern ● CD 06_160

3 Bottle, Chengde Mountain Resort ● CD 06_161

4 Facet of a vase with a zodiac pattern ● CD 06_162

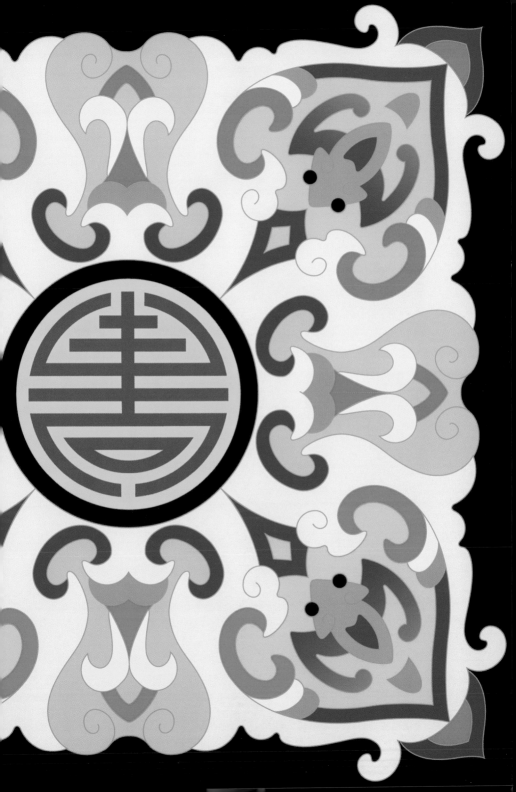

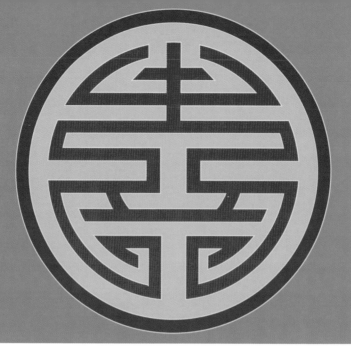

■ Dish with a painted design of "Shou" character of five fortunes ● CD 06_163

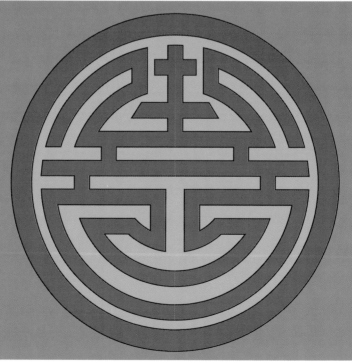

■ Bottle with a painted design of "Shou" character in lotus pattern ● CD 06_164

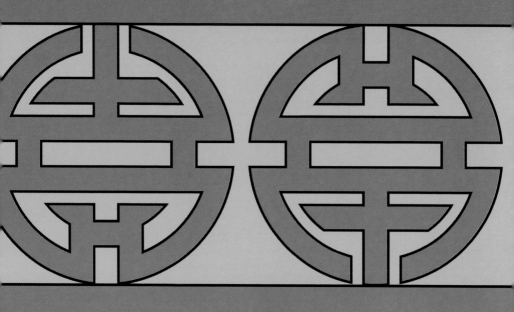

■ Beam of a wooden pagoda ● CD 06_165

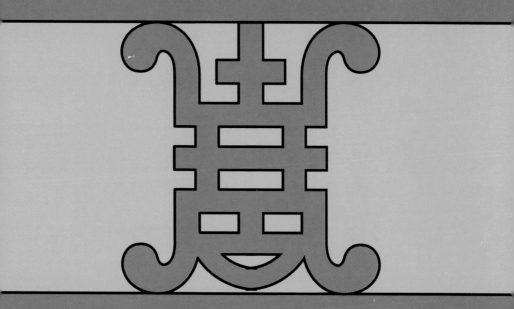

■ Beam of a wooden pagoda ● CD 06_166

● CD 06 167 – 169
Happiness (Ki, Xi)

"Double happiness pattern" now used more than "Longevity"

Two consecutive "喜 happiness" characters is called "Double happiness pattern", and it is categorized as a pattern rather than a character. In addition, the Chinese people regard double "喜 happiness" as a symbol of a happy couple (a couple doubled "喜") and have often use the Double happiness pattern at weddings.

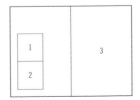

1 Ceiling, Center part ● CD 06_167
2 Dish with painted Xi character in underglaze blue, Yongzheng era (1723~1735) ● CD 06_168
3 Wall ornament of a wooden pagoda ● CD 06_169

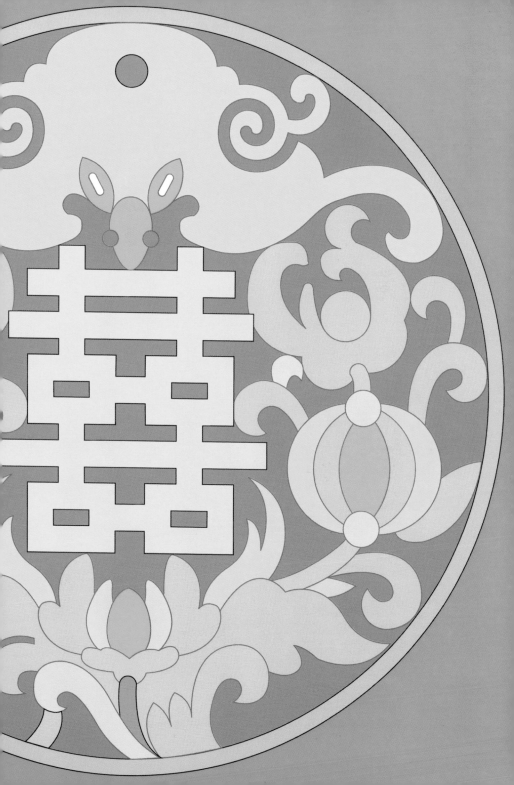

● CD 06 170
Blessing, Good Fortune, Good Luck (fuku/Fu)

"福"not patterned like "寿 Longevity" and "双喜 Double happiness"

When "福 Blessing" is used for ornament, unlike "寿 Longevity" and "喜 Happiness", it is in the form of handwriting in most cases, and its designed pattern is rarely seen. However, it is still a widely known custom to use a paper cutout of the "Blessing" character as a Chinese New Year decoration, or to post a handwritten one upside down on the front door.

*寿・喜・福 1: Chinese characters usually have more then one meaning. As lucky symbols, 寿 stands for longevity, 喜 for happiness, and 福 for blessing. 2: The pronunciation of 寿 is "shou" in Chinese. "Shou" is written in the Chinese spelling system and it is only the phonic part of the character. It also represents other Chinese characters that sound the same. The same is applied to 喜 (Ki, Xi) and 福 (Fuku, Fu).

■ Can with painted "Fu-Shou" characters in underglaze blue, Qing Dynasty ● CD 06_170 This is an example of a wall ornament. The upside-down character of "Blessing" in the red square is written in Small Seal Script.

Chapter 7
Lattice Pattern

⦿ CD 07 171 – 174

Partition/Transom/ Railing – 1

Latticework represents another Chinese sense of beauty

The style of lattice we see at Chinese stores or on furniture is said to have been prefected during the Ming dynasty. While Chinese patterns have gorgeous or, in a sense, excessive decorations, they can also have simple beauty such as that of lattices with straight and curved lines.

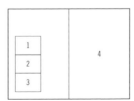

1 2 3 4 ⦿ CD 07_171, 172, 173, 174
These lattice patterns are used to decorate openwork transom between a beam and a nageshi. This is probably the most popular Chinese pattern.

*Nageshi : Non-penetrating tie beams that are made to fit around pillars of temples and shrines.

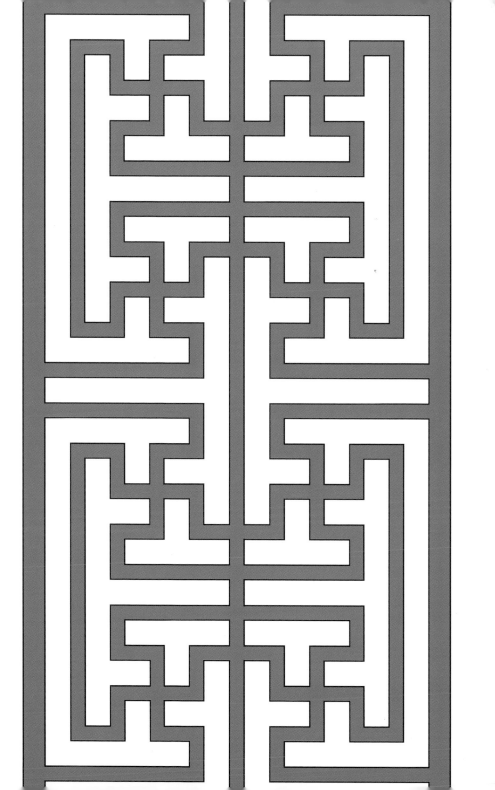

■ ● CD 07_175 ■ ● CD 07_176

This is a simplified lattice pattern used to decorate an openwork transom between a beam and a nageshi*.

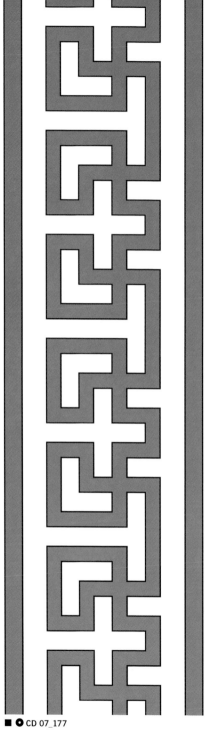

■ ● CD 07_177

■ ● CD 07_178

● CD 07 179 – 181
Partition/Transom/ Railing – 2

Each lattice design with its own pattern

There are numerous lattice designs in furniture and architecture. The number of designs is almost the same as the number of lattice pieces produced over the course of years. There are seemingly infinite designed patterns in China, inlcuding lattices with complicated or delicate patterns, with curved lines, with various local colors that reflect ethnicity, and with concrete images of fortune patterns.

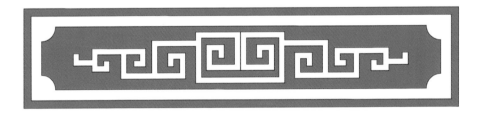

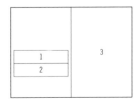

1 2 3 ● CD 07_179, 180, 181
These are latticework to decorate transom. They seem to be not for openwork transom, but for decoration of wooden or plaster walls.

* Kokabe : A long, narrow, horizontal wall above the upper non-penetrating tie beams located between the lintels and ceiling moldings above the transom and above the translucent or opaque sliding screens.

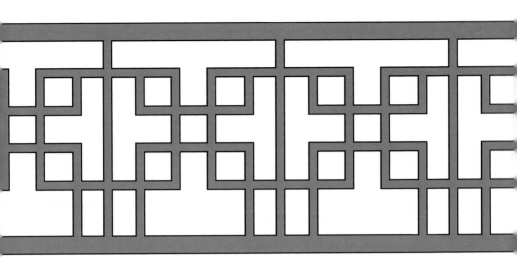

■ ● CD 07_182
This is a complicated pattern work to decorate kokabe*, transom, and railing.

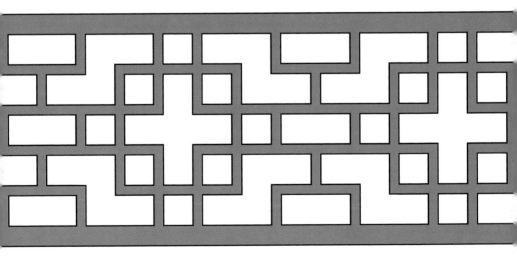

■ ● CD 07_183

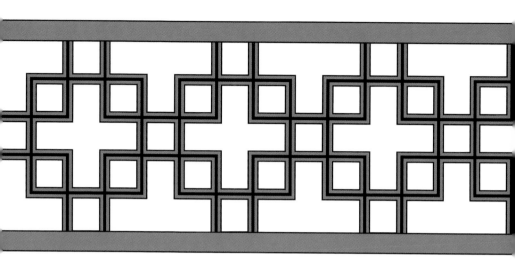

■ ● CD 07_184

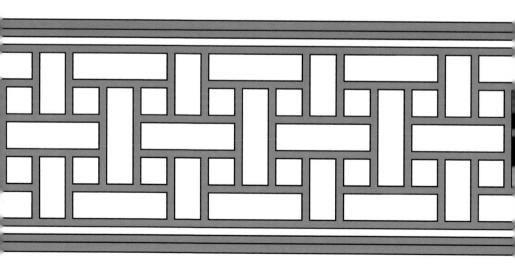

■ ● CD 07_185

● CD 07 186 – 190
Partition/Transom/ Railing – 3

Keeping its quality, the beauty of lattice progressed with limitless patterns

Chinese lattice is generally called "flower board". Those elaborate patterns would be recognized as flowers when seen from a distance. The lattice patterns which I introduced here were made during the Qing dynasty (~AD 1600), judging from their delicate design with gentle curves. They display the technique of pattern variation.

		3
	1	4
	2	
		5

1 2 3 4 5 ● CD 07_186 187 188 189 190
These are considerably elaborate lattices with curved lines. Mainly they are for railings of stairs and corridors.

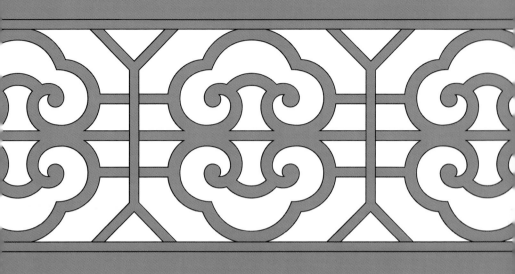

■ ○ CD 07_191 Lattice pattern with curves has an elegant taste. This is probably a railing ornament of a pagoda.

■ ○ CD 07_192

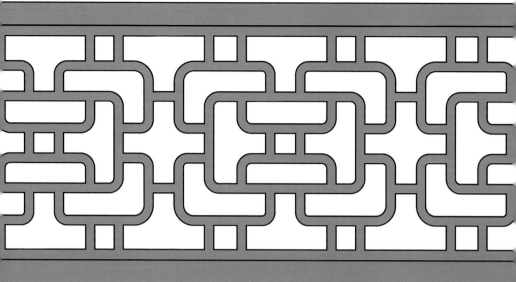

■ ● CD 07_193

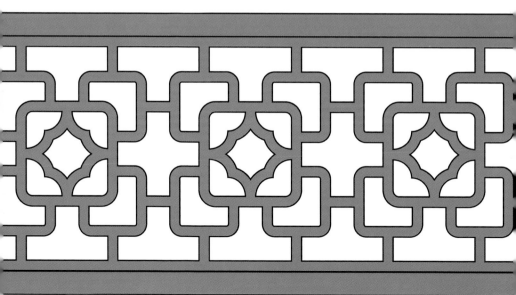

■ ● CD 07_194

■ ● **CD 07_195** The relatively wide latticework is normally used as a dropped wall from the ceiling.

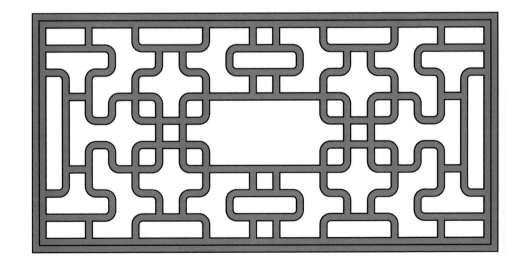

■ ● **CD 07_196**

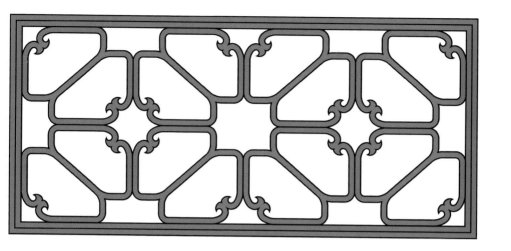

■ ○ CD 07_197

■ ○ CD 07_198

● CD 07 199 – 203
Partition/Transom/ Railing – 4

Chinese architectural ornaments

We Westerners often have an impression that the Chinese way of ornamentation in wooden architecture is to paint in vivid colors or decorate with many carvings. But buildings simply decorated with red lattice exist in China. Though they are simple, they are exquisite.

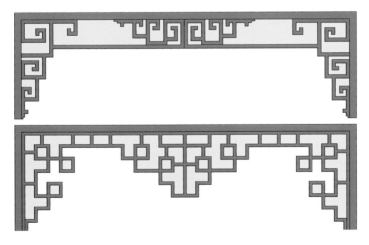

	3
	4
1	
2	5

1 2 3 4 5 ● CD 07_199 200 201 202 203
A gate style ornament from a pillar to another is an openwork dropped wall (lattice). It can be seen from both the inside and the outside of a building.

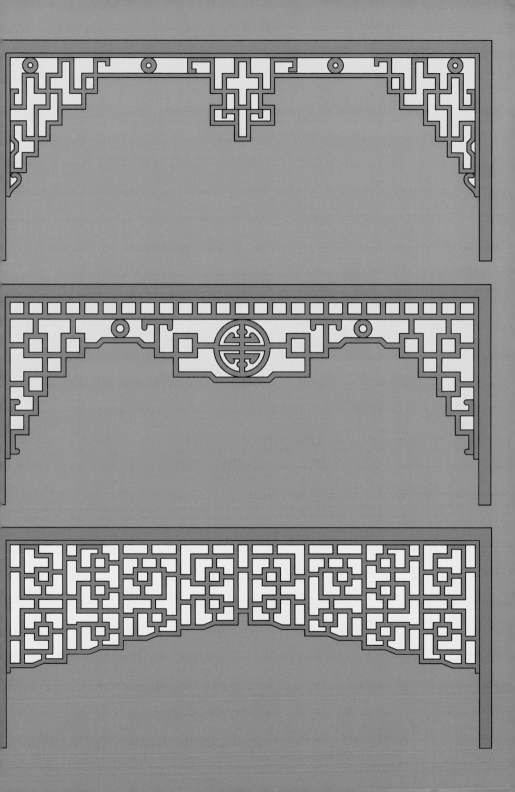

● CD 07 204 – 206
Furniture/Window – 1

"Lattice" as ventilation composed of Buddhism images

Lattice is praised as a masterpiece of wooden framework. When was lattice invented and how was it developed? There is no evidence in the history of Chinese architecture. However, it could have been a simple partition with wooden frames to take in light and wind at first. The lattice patterns probably had developed gradually from reproductions of Buddhism images to delicate wooden frameworks.

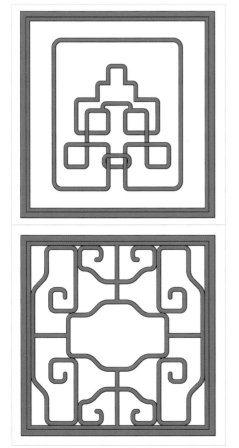

1 2 3 ● CD 07_204 205 206
Some parts clearly took images from flowers at an altar, and the compositions of curves are not commonly seen.

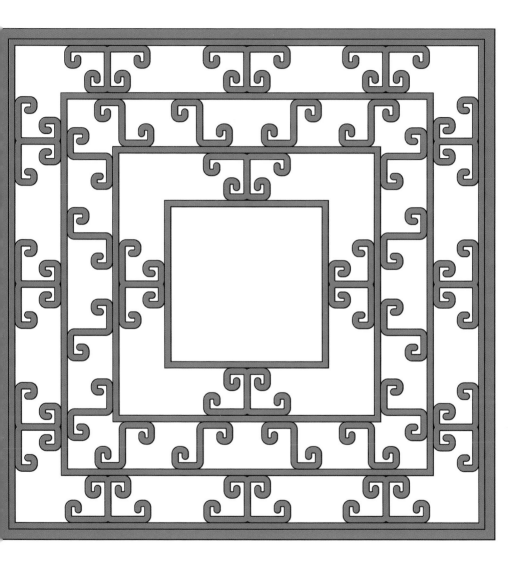

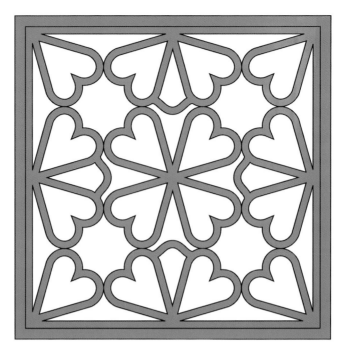

■ ○ **CD 07_207** This lattice pattern seems to have reproduced a Buddhist painting on the ceiling of Mogao caves.

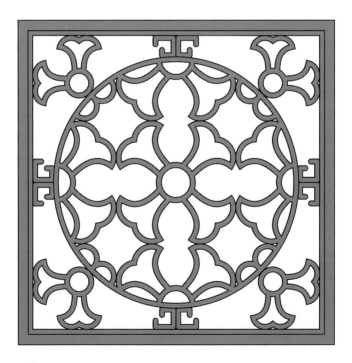

■ ○ CD 07_208

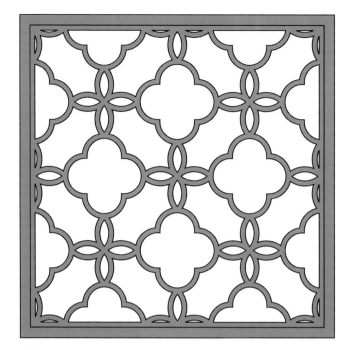

■ ● CD 07_209

■ ● CD 07_210

● CD 07 211 – 214
Furniture/Window – 2

"Lattice" to coordinate the Chinese style of living aesthetically

In the days of Tang (around 600 A.D.), the Chinese people already had a custom of sitting on a chair. Lattice work in architecture must have had something to do with this evolution of lifestyle. It is not a question of which – architecture or lattice pattern to decorate furniture—had developed first. Presumably, the Chinese people tried to coordinate their way of life aesthetically.

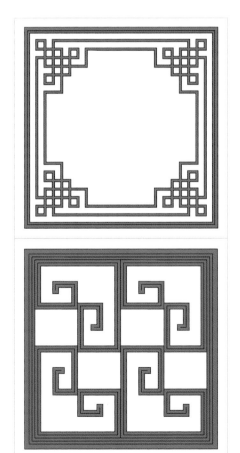

1	3
2	4

1 2 3 4 ● CD 07_211, 212, 213, 214
These are common patterns on furniture such as windows, screens, doors of chests, and chairs.

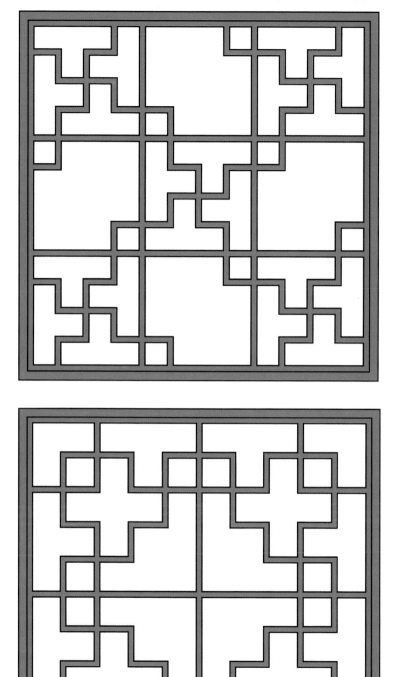

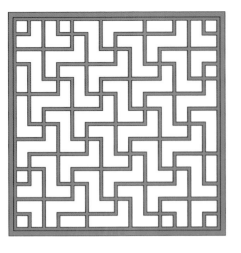

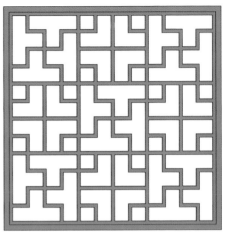

■ ○ CD 07_215
Complicated wastika patterns.

■ ○ CD 07_217

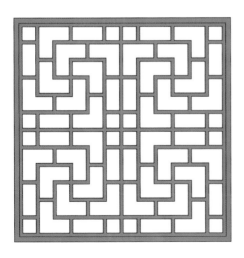

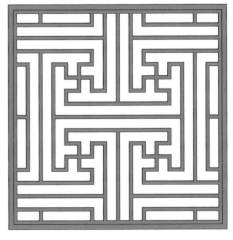

■ ○ CD 07_216

■ ○ CD 07_218

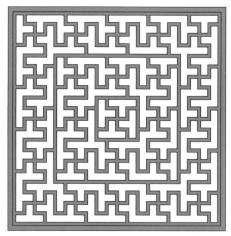

■ ● CD 07_219   ■ ● CD 07_220

■ ● CD 07_221

● CD 07 222 – 225
Furniture/Window – 3

Luxury and gorgeousness of lattice in delicacy not in colors

We tend to relate luxurious gorgeousness to flamboyancy in colors. As for lattice, real beauty lies in the skill of delicate work. Of course, there are some excellent painted lattice windows. Still, elaborately designed pure lattice with wood grain has overwhelming magnificence.

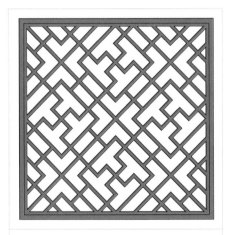

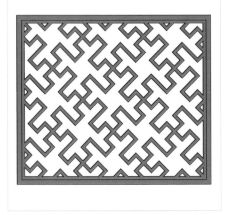

	3
1	
2	4

1 2 3 4 ● CD 07_222, 223, 224, 225
Patterns placed on the bias look even more progressive.

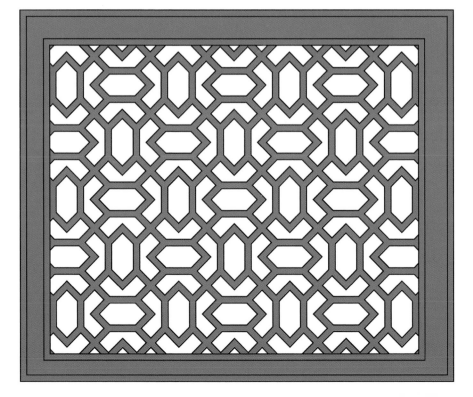

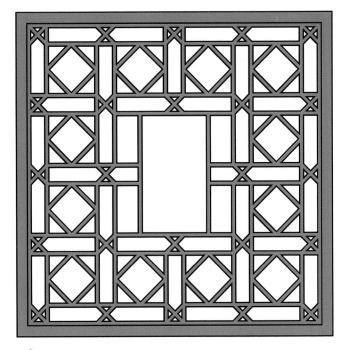

■ ○ **CD 07_226**
This elaborately patterned latticework gives a very elegant and gorgeous impression.

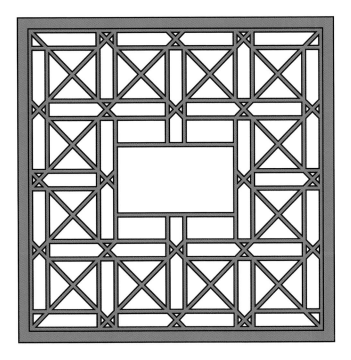

■ ○ **CD 07_227**

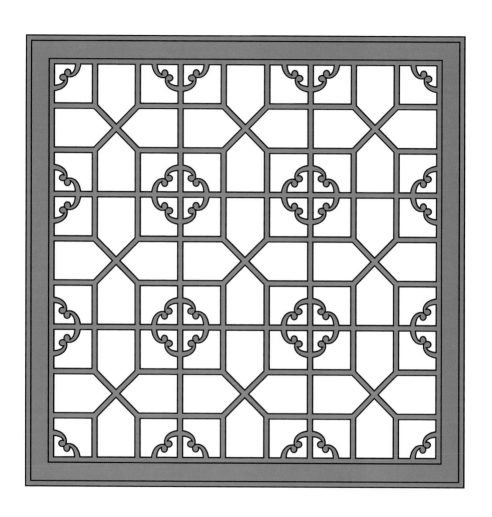

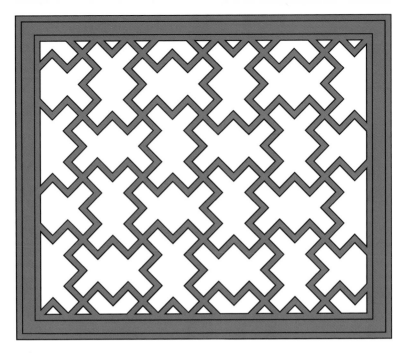

■ ● CD 07_229
This looks like twill pattern on textile. A considerably high skill level would be necessary to make it. It gives us a soft and gentle impression.

■ ● CD 07_230

Chapter 8
Corner Pattern

● CD 08 231 – 234
Wall/Partition lattice – 1

Chinese ornamental patterns produced to reflect social situations and purposes

In China, even the lattice itself keeps some kind of meanings. Chinese national traits of "the narration preference" are well observed in latticework, which reflects social situations and purposes under influences of the times, area, and power. This tendency is common to all Chinese ornament patterns.

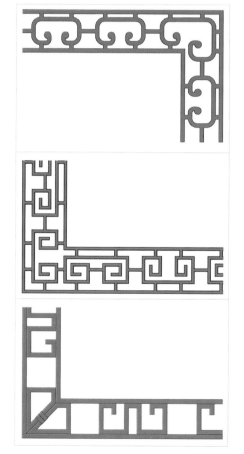

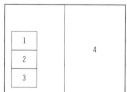

1 **2** **3** **4** Architectural ornaments of wooden temples
● CD 08_231 232 233 234
These corner patterns are applied mainly along pillars and beams of Chinese temples.

■ Architectural ornaments of wooden pagodas ● CD 08_235, 236, 237
These ornaments with concrete patterns were seemingly for pagodas and palaces.

● CD 08 240 – 243
Wall/Partition lattice – 2

Geometrically designed Lattice with less flavor of China

In Chinese latticework, there are some abstract designs that cannot be put in the distintly "Chinese" category. Considering that China is a huge, multiracial nation with a history of 4000 years, there are wide differences in the characteristic of Chinese ornamental art by time period and area. Nevertheless, we have a certain image of "Chinese" style. From that viewpoint, the lattice pieces in this section are abstract and have less of a traditional taste of China.

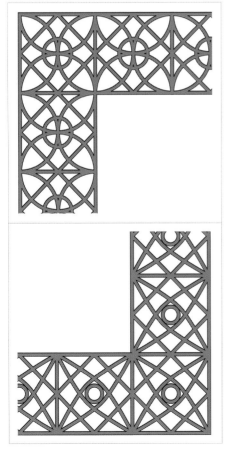

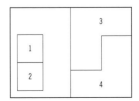

1 2 3 4 Architectural ornaments of pagodas
● CD 08_240, 241, 242, 243
These are very practical patterns just like a mathematical model. Infinite original patterns can be made by simplifying these patterns.

● CD 08 244 – 246
Ceiling

Mysterious ceiling paintings with complications of various motifs

The ceiling paintings of the Mogao Caves are composed of various shapes and motifs, and their mysterious world enchants anyone who sees them. The corner ornaments consist of motifs different from those of the center part of the ceiling. However, the paintings are consonant in coloring and design like, as it were, heavenly music. Even from the corner ornaments, the harmonious world of the painting can be imagined. In addition, corner parts by themselves also make perfect designs.

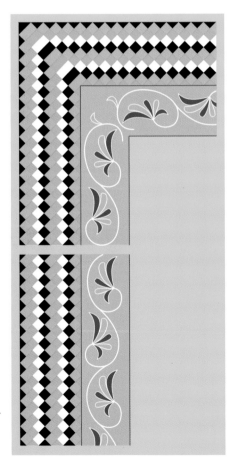

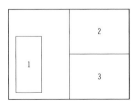

1 2 3 Ceiling paintings at the Mogao Caves. Part of corner ornament ● CD 08_244, 245, 246
Though inspired by Buddhist art, these patterns developed their own universal elements.

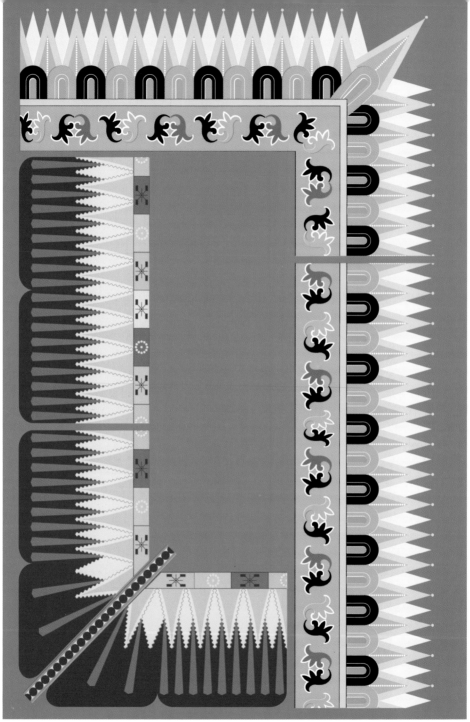

■ Ceiling paintings at the Mogao Caves. Part of corner ornament ◉ CD 08_247, 248
These patterns with geometric straight lines are simple and well balanced.

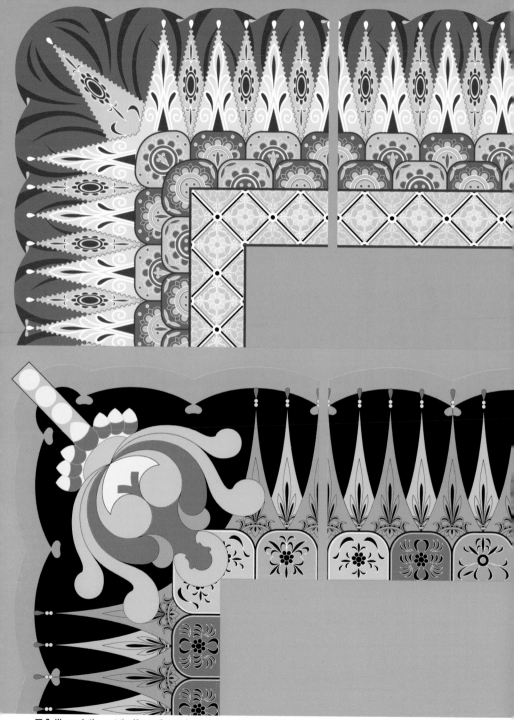

■ Ceiling paintings at the Mogao Caves. Part of corner ornament ⬤ CD 08_249, 250

[About the Author]
Shigeki Nakamura An art director since 1964, he established Cobble Corporation Co. Ltd. in 1987. The company published a book of ESP Pattern Library Digital Materials, which can be seen on its website (http://www.cobbleart.com/). He has received many awards, such as the Minister of International Trade and Industry Award, and he is a member of the JAGDA (Japanese Graphic Designer Association).